The Be-Attitudes

Reflections on the Beatitudes

By Sri Swami Satchidananda

Cover Art

By Peter Max

T0025524

Library of Congress Cataloging in
Publication Data
Satchidananda, Swami.
The Be-Attitudes: Reflections on the Beatitudes

I. Title.
2022
IBSN 978-0-932040-09-1

Printed in the United States of America.

Integral Yoga® Publications
Satchidananda Ashram–Yogaville, Inc.
108 Yogaville Way, Buckingham, VA, USA 23921
www.integralyoga.org

Books by
Sri Swami Satchidananda

Beyond Words

Enlightening Tales

The Golden Present

Bound To Be Free:
The Liberating Power
of Prison Yoga

Heaven on Earth

Integral Yoga Hatha

Kailash Journal

The Living Gita

To Know Your Self

Yoga Sutras of Patanjali

The Yoga Way

Titles in this special
Peter Max cover art series:

Meditation

The Key to Peace

Overcoming Obstacles

Adversity and Awakening

Satchidananda Sutras

Gems of Wisdom

Pathways to Peace

How to Find Happiness

The Be-Attitudes

Everything Will Come to You

Thou Art That

Golden Moments

Free Yourself

The Guru Within

Books/Films about
Sri Swami Satchidananda

Sri Swami Satchidananda:
  Biography of a Yoga Master

Sri Swami Satchidananda:
  Portrait of a Modern Sage

The Master's Touch

Boundless Giving: The Life and Service of
  Sri Swami Satchidananda

Living Yoga: The Life and Teachings of
  Swami Satchidananda (digital video)

Many Paths, One Truth: The Interfaith
  Message of Swami Satchidananda (DVD)

The Essence of Yoga:
  The Path of Integral Yoga with
  Swami Satchidananda (DVD)

In the Footsteps of a Master:
  The 1970 World Peace Tour with Swami
  Satchidananda (DVD)

For a complete listing of books, CDs and DVDs:
  www.iydbooks.com

Acknowledgments

Integral Yoga® Publications is grateful to be able to offer this newly expanded version of a small booklet printed in 1974 that was originally titled: *Blessed are They*. A loving and reverential deep bow to our beloved Gurudev, Sri Swami Satchidananda, for these inspiring and illuminating teachings. Our thanks to Swami Hamsananda, Rev. Parvathi Moore and others who have transcribed many of the talks given by Sri Gurudev; to Swami Murugananda for creating and maintaining the transcribed talks archive. Thanks also to Swami Hamsananda for copyediting and to Swami Premananda for editing and for project management of this edition.

Our gratitude to Peter (Atman) Max, for the beautiful artwork that adorns the cover, to Victor (Arjuna) Zurbel for the cover design, and Shiva Herve for the layout. Without the support of generous donors like the Harry Wadhwani family, Rev. Sivani Alderman, and the Mahesh Daswani family, the Peter Max Special Cover Art Series would not have been possible.

Contents

Foreword

By Brother David Steindl-Rast, OSB

Swami Satchidananda (whom I affectionately call "Swamiji," and who lovingly refers to me as "his brother, David") rightly says that all spiritual paths lead to the one Truth.

It strains our imagination, but we must even say that taking one path means taking all of them—they are all contained in each. Yet, this will help us not in the least until we set out to make one path our own and follow it.

To really follow what Yoga offers us for a deeper understanding of Christian teaching, we must begin to live what Christ teaches. How else should we understand its meaning? Why not let these two spiritual paths—two ways of expression—complement one another?

To get at the truth, we must make every effort to understand what the one who used these words wanted to say at the time. The longer ago this was, the greater our difficulty today yet, difficult or not, every statement of truth has to be seen in its context.

A given perspective always allows us to see certain things more clearly than others; and the perspective of this or that tradition allows us to express certain aspects of truth more clearly than others. Two languages might, if we are lucky, complement each other as two pictures taken in different perspectives complement each other, or two kinds of food together bring out one another's finest flavor.

It is in this sense that one might find in Yoga a kind of key to understanding Christianity and vice-versa too, we may hope. And, this is what Swami Satchidananda offers us through his teachings: a way to access the deepest wisdom from within whatever tradition or spiritual path we may walk.

Reading the signposts isn't easy, whether they are koans, passages from the *Bible*, from the *Vedas*, or from any other sacred tradition. One has to learn the language of that particular tradition. Moreover, this language changes in the course of time, so that the truth has to be restated in contemporary language when its expression has become obsolete.

This is also what Swamiji does so well in translating, interpreting, and sharing teaching stories and parables.

Yoga, at its best, truly gives expression to that awareness of universal communion that is so basic to our spiritual experience: in the very act of knowing God, it is God, the unknown Knower, who knows in us; God is our innermost self, the true Self in us all.

There is no inner contradiction between the mystic who says. "I know that I am God" and the mystic who hears God saying. "I am the one who is; you are the one who is not." The apparent contradiction arises from the limitations of language and perspective. You can only say one thing at a time; you have to choose your point of view. But the experience of the mystics and our own deepest experience reveals that the opposites coincide in God.

Spiritual experience remains the touchstone for spiritual doctrine. And our spiritual experience, where it is most genuine, brings home to us both our oneness with God and our spontaneous gratitude for this gift.

Jesus says that the Kingdom of God, our ultimate joy and salvation, is here—a totally gratuitous gift, the discovery of a treasure for which we didn't even look; a pot of gold hit by the plow in our own field. "The Kingdom of God is in the midst of you. And yet it is like a pearl from far distant shores, so precious that it costs no less than everything" (Luke, 17:20).

Yoga—as you will see Swamiji describe in this book—teaches us the same truth found in the Beatitude: "Blessed are the pure in heart, for they shall see God." We can and must affirm how our spiritual traditions enrich each other when viewed from the perspective Swamiji shares with us. We affirm our traditions by a life that remains grateful.

In that deep gratitude, which is an essential characteristic of our peak moments, we experience one common denominator to all the spiritual paths: that we can't wrap up the light in a package; but we can walk in the light.

Introduction

When Yoga master Swami Satchidananda (known as Sri Gurudev to his students) arrived in Europe, and later, the United States, he recognized that the majority of people followed the Christian faith.

He felt the teachings of Yoga that he was bringing from India could be made more accessible to westerners through some bridge-building. So, he spent time studying the *Bible* and the teachings of Jesus Christ and finding the common boundaries between Yoga and Christianity.

In doing so he gained even more of an appreciation and reverence for Jesus and he discovered a very deep resonance between the Beatitudes (in the "Sermon on the Mount") and teachings in the *Yoga Sutras of Patanjali*, a foundational text of classical Yoga.

One Beatitude in particular captured Sri Gurudev's attention and his heart: "Blessed are the pure in heart, for they shall see God." In so many of his public talks he would speak about this Beatitude and he would point out the similarity of the profound teaching with the goal of Yoga expressed in *sutras* 1.2 and 1.3 of the *Yoga Sutras*:

"'Blessed are the pure in heart, for they shall see God" is almost an exact translation of the goal of Yoga given in *sutra* 1.2, '*Yogas chitta vritti nirodhah*.' The translation is: 'Yoga is the stilling of the thought-waves in the mind.'

"If we use the biblical language for this *sutra*, we could say: Blessed are those who have eliminated the *vrittis* (thought-waves) in the *chitta* (mind). *Sutra* 1.3 is '*Tada drashtuh svarupe'vasthanam*,' meaning: 'Then the seer rests in its own True Nature.'

"We can see this *sutra* translated in the second half of the Beatitudes, for when we rest in our True Nature we are in God. So, in a way, this Beatitude is very similar to Patanjali's aim behind Yoga."

At Satchidananda Ashram–Yogaville in Connecticut in the mid-1970s, Sri Gurudev would often come and give *satsang* to those living at the Ashram, including guests and visitors. *Satsang* is a Sanskrit word that means "company of the wise."

Satsang takes place whenever spiritual seekers gather together to receive and to share in spiritual teachings. While sometimes these *satsangs* at the Ashram were scheduled, often they would take place spontaneously and unexpectedly.

During one such occasion, Sri Gurudev dropped in at the time of the regular Friday evening program during which scriptures and sacred texts were studied. On this occasion, the scripture being studied was the *Bible*. The plan had been to read the first twelve verses, the Beatitudes, from St. Matthew, Chapter 5.

Sri Gurudev was delighted to hear this and joined the gathering of students. These students took the opportunity to ask him if they could read each Beatitude and receive his insights about it, particularly from a yogic view.

He agreed and the *satsang* was recorded and transcribed. This book is the text of that *satsang*, with additional text from other talks he gave over the years.

Chapter 1: The Poor in Spirit

Blessed are the poor in spirit, for theirs is the kingdom of heaven.

Swami Satchidananda:

What is meant when Jesus uses the words "poor in spirit?" Had he just said, "the poor," we might assume he was talking about poverty and that he was advising us not to have any money or possessions so that we may enjoy the kingdom of heaven. But, he was not talking about material poverty or about leaving everything and running away to a cave.

Someone may be "rich" even if they have only a small begging bowl to which they are attached. Spirit is actually the feeling, not in material things outside. So the real "poverty of spirit" means to deeply feel that you are not attached to anything and to not define who you are by what you have or what you do.

We should understand this point in the proper light. When we talk about leading a life of non-attachment or non-clinging, some people misunderstand and think it means to simply not care about anything or anyone. No, non-attachment or dispassion doesn't mean disinterest in life but, rather, not clinging to things as a means of being happy. Detachment means a type of relationship to the world and to people that is not based on self-centeredness.

Everyone has certain responsibilities in their lives and part of those include associating with various people and things. For example, suppose you have a bank teller as your friend. You go to the bank one day to see your friend because you need some money. You walk into the bank, go up to their window and you see they have thousands of dollars around them.

You say, "Hey, I need a hundred dollars urgently, can you give me some of the money in your drawer there?" What would they say? Even though your friend seems to have so many bundles of hundred-dollar bills, they tell you, "Sorry, I don't have any money I can give you." What does it mean?

Even though they have so much cash in the drawer next to them, they know it doesn't belong to them. They realize that money is not theirs and so they are not attached to that. That friend is only handling the money as part of their duties. In the same way, even though we have all the power of position, family, friends, and everything, we must realize they are all God-sent. We only have certain responsibilities toward them—to love and serve them in the proper way—not to *own* them.

There is nothing that we can call "ours" so, in this way, we can avoid all the egoism and ego-identification and that is what is meant by real poverty. You know that nothing belongs to you—things come and they will be there as long as you are using them. At a certain point, they'll just go away. They are given to you and they are taken back.

I will give you another simple example. I just walked into the *satsang* hall and I saw there was a seat for me to sit in, a microphone in front, and now I am using it. I have no right to misuse it; I have no right to possess it. When I finish speaking with you all, if I just pick up the microphone, take it off the stand, put it in my pocket and go, what will you think of me? Everything is here in life for our use, so that we may be of service, not so we can possess it. This is the attitude in life we can have toward everyone and everything.

Just today when I was walking toward the Ashram garage, I saw a young man who was new to the Ashram. He remarked, "I feel so peaceful and so comfortable here. It's so nice to be out of the material world." And I asked him, "What do you mean? You *are* in the material world here. Here is the Ashram garage with all tools, screwdrivers, hammers, and maintenance equipment. Yet, you are saying that you are away from the material world. We have all the materials here. But somehow you feel that you are away from the material world and you are more peaceful and comfortable. So that is the proof that it is not the materials that make the material world. The materials are innocent. They don't affect you if you have the proper relationship with them."

That is why I'm saying that even if you have all the wealth in the world around you, you can still be "poor in spirit" if you are not attached to that. On the other hand, even if you are in a cave or in a tent, if you are still attached to those you are not poor in spirit.

It is not the *things* that make you poor or rich, it is the *attitude*. So that is why this Beatitude says, "Blessed are the poor in spirit." It doesn't say, "Blessed are the poor in material." Poor in material is totally different.

A person who has no money, no proper clothing to wear, no house, and so on, is poor in material. But poverty in spirit must be well-understood. Spiritual poverty means that your spirit is not affected by any attachments; you are not identified with what you have. You know that you have things, you know you have a certain role and responsibilities, and you recognize those are not your true identity. Knowing who you are and being established in your essential nature is what is meant by being "blessed" and to have the "kingdom of heaven."

What is your essential nature? Your True Nature is Divine. Divine or Cosmic Consciousness is the ultimate reality and each of us is the same Light of Consciousness appearing in different forms. To realize this and to recognize your essential nature takes total renunciation of any selfish attitude in life and any identification with a false identity.

When you have renounced personal attachment and clinging to a false identity, your mind will be calm and clean because it is the clinging that disturbs the mind. Then you are truly blessed.

Chapter 2: The Mourners

Blessed are they that mourn, for they shall be comforted.

Swami Satchidananda:

Why do we normally mourn? Because we've lost something. So it may sound strange if you say, "I'm mourning" and someone tells you, "You are blessed." You won't even want to hear this. Yet, there is a very important life teaching here: Suffering brings a blessing.

What is the blessing? The great South Indian sage Thiruvalluvar explained that the more we suffer, the more we get purified. Often pain comes because we are sad, depressed, or mourning something we lost to which we were attached. It could be a loved one, a job, a friend, and so on. It doesn't mean we shouldn't mourn losses. Jesus didn't say, "Blessed are they who don't mourn." It's natural to mourn a loss or experience sadness and grief. It's also an opportunity to reflect on our relationship to people and things. Caring and loving someone or something is natural; clinging and selfish attachment is not.

Remember that there is nothing that is permanent in this world. Don't we say that the only thing we know for certain is that we will all die one day? When you get something, you will have to lose it one day or another. Because something came to you, it will also go. When it comes to you, welcome and celebrate that. And when it goes, celebrate the farewell.

The truth is that the more you lose, the more you learn to know what the one thing is that can never be lost—call it God, your own divine Self, the inner peace that is your true nature, or whatever name you wish to use. We will lose everything and anything we have gotten.

But, you can't lose something that is already and always there. So the pain that comes from clinging and attachment teaches us to truly value what we can never lose. We have a saying that, "Adversities are blessings in disguise." It sounds crude, unpleasant to the ear. But, there is a great truth in this. Adversities draw out our inner capabilities. And, we gain great understanding, wisdom, and inner strength through adversity.

We don't have to go and look for suffering but we can accept the pain that comes as a learning opportunity and a kind of purification. You don't have to go and purposely put your finger into the fire, no.

Pain and suffering come as a natural part of life. When it comes receive it saying, "Ah, yes, good friend. You have come, thank you. Welcome." When you have this attitude, you will feel comforted, you will feel at peace because you know there is a benefit.

When painful challenges don't come for a while you should wonder, *What's happening to me? Nobody seems to be criticizing me?* Yes. If people always say nice things and everything is always going your way, beware. There is a danger behind this.

Once there was a saint, he was covered with a lot of festering wounds and they started even creating worms inside. And he said, "Okay, God, probably that is the way you are taking away, eating my karma away. Okay." Why did he say this? Because he knew the truth—the purpose of suffering. In this Beatitude, Jesus is teaching us this truth.

The moment you get into Yoga you are getting into a frying pan. The purpose of your practices is to remove any selfishness, smooth out all the wrinkles, change the wrong attitudes and judgments in the mind. Don't ever come to Yoga thinking, *Oh, it's all wonderful, it's going to be smooth and nic*e. You would be mistaken.

After all, what is pain? Pain, loss, suffering are not something that should terrify us. The moment we are frightened of them, then it pains us more. When we are afraid of something, it becomes an even bigger thing to us.

Instead, learn to be fearless. How will that fearlessness come? By having faith. Faith and fear can never go together. When you know that you are in God's hands and that everything is happening to help, not harm you, you will never be afraid of anything. We can't say we believe in God and then not have trust in God. Even our ordinary money seems to have that trust!

One of the South Indian saints said, "I'm not afraid of anything or anybody in this life, not even the death. Why? Because there is somebody who is taking care of me. I have that total trust. I have taken refuge in God so who can do anything to me?"

Remember, we all have to face adversities. It's usually when we have some crisis in our lives that we turn to God or even think of a Higher Power. Why? Because we realize our limitations.

What greater comfort can there be than having that full faith and trust? And that is why if you understand this Beatitude, you will never be afraid of pain. If it comes you will accept it, "Yes, my friend, come. You're coming to help me." Then, you will feel blessed and comforted.

A comforted mind is a peaceful mind. The purpose of Yoga is a peaceful mind. A peaceful mind clearly reflects your true nature so you are better able to recognize this. When you lose your selfish attachments to everything you find that inner peace and tranquility that has always been in you, as you. There is no greater comfort than this.

Chapter 3: The Meek

Blessed are the meek, for they shall inherit the earth.

Swami Satchidananda:

Who are the meek? The ones who are free from egoism. The one who is free from domination by the ego is the one who is free from all the selfishness and that is what meekness refers to here.

Being meek often implies that someone is cowardly or submissive. They seem to have no backbone, are weak, and may be easily pushed around, but this is not the way the term is utilized in this Beatitude.

The use of the word "meek" here is a reference to humility. When the ego becomes free of its self-centeredness, its selfishness, our real spirit and strength can emerge and then we can truly receive all the necessities in life.

Some may misunderstand humility as some kind of inferiority complex. It doesn't mean to lose hope, to belittle yourself, and make you fit for nothing Some people go to the extent of feeling, *Oh, I am hopeless, I'm not fit for anything*. That is not actually humility.

Humility is understanding that what we each have is very little in comparison to the Infinite. And unless we are humble, unless we bend down, or put ourselves below the Giver, we can't receive. Who is that Giver? God. We give ourselves to the Giver in humility and what do we get in return? We inherit the earth. We are children of God and loving children will inherit everything from their Mother/Father/God.

That's why if we go in front of the altar, where we see God reflected, we bow down. We kneel down and in some places around the world, people even prostrate. Without that feeling of humility and gratitude, we can't receive much. Always, the receiving hand comes below the giving hand. That is humility and it is always combined with a sense of gratitude.

Humility is a great virtue. Even if a person knows a lot, they can be humble. In fact, the person who knows more, will always feel more humble. They understand that there is much more to learn because there is no limit for learning, no limit for knowing.

Scientifically, knowledge flows like any other energy. For example, liquid flows from a higher level to the lower level. If you want to fill an empty gas can with gas, the empty can has to stay below the gas pump. If by any chance the empty can goes above the pump, what happens? Nothing flows. It is the same for human beings who want to receive spiritual knowledge and blessings.

In the spiritual sense, the biggest block keeping us from receiving—or "inheriting the earth," as Jesus said—is the egocentric feeling of "I," as in "I know everything, I must be in control, I will get whatever I want." The self-centered "I, me, mine" is the basic veil between the True Self and the ego. So, the entire process of *sadhana* (spiritual practice) is to clean up the selfish ego. Once that ego becomes clean, then it doesn't stop the flow of the Pure Consciousness to the purified ego.

This is an important point because what we want is a purified ego, not to destroy the ego. Even to say, "I'm getting rid of" or "I'm destroying my ego" is a part of ego! We can't destroy the ego and we shouldn't.

If you don't have that incentive, that ego, you can't even work on your ego. That means, you take a cleaner, less problematic part of the ego to work on the main part of the ego that needs to be cleaned up.

Something like when a parent is busy, they might ask the older child to do some washing, change the baby's diaper, and things like that. We need the ego to help us in many ways. So we utilize a part of the ego to clean up the other part. What is the best way to clean the ego? By humbling oneself.

One of the great qualities of a true spiritual seeker is humility. To be always humble. Because without that you cannot clean the ego. It will try to pop out every minute. It will look for opportunities to assert its domination. But, when you cultivate humility you are doing something beautiful, something to clean your ego, and if you keep on doing it you get the benefit.

I like to give the example of cleaning a dirty cloth. How do you do that? You buy another piece of dirt, a good smelling dirt. Then, you apply that to the dirty cloth and the good dirt knows how to play with the old dirt and they get churned up together in the washer until the undesirable dirt forgets to cling onto the cloth.

At just the right time in the rinse and spin cycle, both the old dirt and the new dirt you added are eliminated. They both get rinsed out and you are left with a clean cloth.

All our spiritual practices are the soap we add to the water and then ultimately the entire ego becomes clean. When this happens, instead of identifying with the ego, which is only a tool to help us, we are able to recognize our True Self in the way that Jesus explained, "I and my Father are one."

As the Old Testament also taught, "God made man in His own Image," or as we say in Sanskrit: "*Sivoham Soham.* I am that Pure Auspiciousness, Divine Consciousness." When you can recognize this Truth, you not only "inherit the earth" but also the "kingdom of heaven."

Chapter 4: The Righteous

Blessed are they which do hunger and thirst after righteousness, for they shall be filled.

Sri Swami Satchidananda:

Righteousness has several different meanings that are all interconnected, among them: seeking Truth and wisdom, being dedicated to a Higher Power and higher purpose, living a virtuous and selfless life.

What is Truth then? Anything that is universal, infinite, that is true in all times, places, and circumstances and can never be destroyed. If it comes today and it disappears tomorrow, it's not absolute Truth. Anything that has a form and a name doesn't stay as it is. A bunch of grain changes into a cake. The cake changes into some kind of pulp when consumed. And that changes into some energy or blood when digested, while the rest changes into something else that is thrown out. So this grain, the cake, the energy, are all the changes of one stuff that keeps on changing.

Here is another example: There is water in the sea. Do you see anything else in the sea? When you go to the ocean you might say, "Oh, look at that wave. Look at that iceberg. Look at that spray. Look at that bubble." You call them differently but essentially there is only one truth: they are all water. The names and forms change, but the essential nature, water, never changes. In the same way, you were a baby, then you began to grow into a young person, and later into an adult. Still later, you become old and eventually die. But throughout that process, *you*, your essential nature, never changed. Your body kept on changing and you got different labels.

What is our essential nature? We are made in the image of God; we are divine by nature but because we always live at the level of the body, mind, and intellect, we forget our spiritual essence. The entire universe is nothing but name and form and behind the names and forms the essence is the same. That is the truth, the eternal truth, and that never changes. Truth is not limited by a form or a name, so it is just the essence. It has not appeared as a thing or an object. But behind everything, there is the essence. We may call this essence as God, Truth, inner peace, True Nature, the light of Consciousness, and so on.

Even though we see many things and, for convenience's sake, call them by different names and forms, everything is made out of the same essence, or are the expressions of the same essence. In that way, we can see the diversity without missing the unity. The unity, or the essence, is the Truth. That one essence is expressed in form as the many, as the diversity we see in the material world. The many expressions of the one essence are to be enjoyed as part of the play of the Divine. If all these names and forms dissolved, then there'd be just the Cosmic Essence. What fun would we have then? Imagine a big piece of cardboard:

you cut it into small pieces that are all blank. Where is the play? Now, print colors there, put clubs, diamonds, spades, hearts and then put numbers, queen, jack, ace, everything. And then you shuffle them and play. Now you can really enjoy the fun.

That's why I always say that when we remember that in essence we are all one we can enjoy the diversity without any problems. When we forget the unity and only see the diversity then we fight over what religion is better, what country is better, what race is better, and so on. Then we get caught in it and don't play anymore. We get strangulated and suffer.

So, blessed are the people who keep an eye on the basic Truth; they will have all fun. Yes! Because the person who knows how to play without forgetting the Truth enjoys fun always. Blessed are the people who rise above the changing phenomena and who realize the unchanging One.

Now, coming to hunger and thirst. Jesus is telling us that we should be after Truth, after righteousness, like someone who is hungering and thirsting for food and water. They are starving, they are parched and they are not just sitting back thinking, *Hmm, what should I eat or drink*? No, they are devotedly yearning, longing, and seeking after righteousness. And when this happens, they are "filled."

Does this remind you of a Sanskrit word in a *sloka* that we repeat at the end of our meditations? *Purnam. Purnam* is fullness, completeness. If you are seeking after righteousness, if you are after the Truth, and if you are really experiencing that Truth, you are full. You have allowed the fullness of God to flow through you. And that fullness never gets depleted. It's like lighting an unlit candle from a lit candle. Does the lit candle loose it's brightness when the unlit candle gets lit? No. In the same way, when we recognize the fullness of God within us, we will never feel empty but will be ever-full.

How would you live your life then? You will live a yogic life based on ethical principles and the spirit of selfless service. My Guru, Sri Swami Sivananda, used to say, "I can comfortably summarize all the scriptural teachings in just two phrases: Be good. Do good. So, serve all, love all, be good to others and do good." It's a simple teaching but if you can just follow this in your life, everything will happen naturally. Remember, Yoga practice is not only when you do *asana*, *pranayama*, or you go and sit and meditate. See that your entire life is permeated with the yogic teachings.

Clean up your body, clean up your mind, express that godliness from within. That is the Truth, that is your essence-nature. Your essential nature is like a diamond. Nobody needs to put the brilliance into the diamond, it's there already. Remove all the rough surface, polish it, it reflects the light. Likewise if you polish yourself, you will reflect and express your inner light in everything you do.

Chapter 5: The Merciful

Blessed are the merciful, for they shall obtain mercy.

Sri Swami Satchidananda:

Saint Francis taught this Beatitude in his beautiful prayer when he said, "It is in pardoning that we are pardoned." What you give you get. If you pardon others' mistakes, yours will be pardoned. If you pardon your debtors, your debts will be pardoned.

Only a pure heart, a selfless heart, can be merciful. A self-absorbed person won't hesitate to harm others to fulfill their own selfishness. So, a merciful attitude is based on selflessness.

God's nature is selfless, that's why we say "God is all-merciful." And if you are merciful, if you are selfless, you are blessed.

That's why the most important thing is to make the mind selfless, make the mind clean and compassionate. See that the mind loves everybody as yourself. If you are completely free from selfishness, you don't have to kill anybody, you don't have to hurt anybody, you don't have to steal anybody's property.

Jesus wants us to be selfless, to be compassionate, and to be kind to everybody— even to love our enemy. And, it is not just Jesus who asks this of us, no religion ever asked us to hate anybody, to dislike anybody.

All spiritual teachings say that if anybody hurts you, forgive and forget. Why? Because if you are going to keep on thinking of those hurts and resentments, you are saturating your system with those feelings.

Remember, the physical body gets nourished by your physical food and your mental-emotional body gets nourished by your thoughts. Thoughts are the food for the mind.

So, if you keep on developing hateful and resentful thoughts, you are nurturing your mind with those thoughts. Yoga tells us to cultivate a clean mind, a peaceful mind.

As we will see in the next Beatitude, Jesus says, "Blessed are the pure in heart, for they shall see God." Purity of heart means a peaceful, tranquil heart. And tranquility of heart cannot be obtained if you develop hatred, dislikes, resentments, and even greed. Craving, aversion, distress, and depression will all disturb the mind.

Instead, we should cultivate positive qualities of compassion, forgiveness, and love. In our world—now more than ever—we need to have a steady, calm, and clean mind and a loving and compassionate heart. So many people are in pain, so many have lost loved ones, and so many are overcome with fear. We need to feel compassion and lovingkindness toward everyone.

In order to cultivate compassion, mercy and forgiveness we need understanding. Why would we have resentment toward someone? Resentment and anger are probably due to our own expectations. For example, *I wanted so-and-so to do this and that or to be this way or that way*. In other words, you had some type of expectation. If I expect a little child to run in the 400-meter race and get the gold medal in the Olympic games and if the child cannot do that should I resent them?

So, you have to understand, *That is the way they are now. They need to mature more in order to race. I would have done the same thing at their age and if someone got angry with me because I couldn't win the race, how would I have felt?* That is the understanding we need. Think in those terms and then you will feel sympathetic toward that person. You will show compassion.

The truth is that people do the best they can do with the maturity and understanding they have. When we understand that, instead of getting resentful and angry, we will probably go and help that person if we can. Resentment is caused by our expectations. *I wanted that to happen but it didn't*. Or, *I wanted that person to do this for me but they didn't.* Or, *Because of that person's interference I didn't get what I wanted.* See? It's all self-centered thinking. Your selfishness causes anger and resentment. On the other hand, think of that person's good qualities.

A person might have been good to you, helped you over the years. One day they would have refused to help you or maybe they hurt you in some way. What happens? You forget all the good days. You remember this one only, *Look what they did to me! I hate them!* Finished. All the good things have gone down in the drain.

Certainly they must have done at least some nice things to you. And even if they never did or they hurt you in some way, forgive them. Think like that. It's unfortunate that they acted that way. You don't ever have to be around them in the future, but don't hold any resentment in your heart. There is a quote in the South Indian sacred text, the *Thirukkural* about this. It says, "If you are a good person and if somebody helps you in even a little, minute way, you should take it as a great gift that you got from them. It's never good to forget someone's good deed, but it is the best way to forget anyone's bad deed."

That's what. Immediately forget it. Don't even keep a bad deed in mind for the next hour or next day. Remember good deeds always. Forget bad deeds immediately. Then you will have no reason for resentment or anger.

And, remember that by your resentment and anger you are not going to get anything. Instead, that is going to spoil your own body and mind. People with resentment and anger will fall sick quickly, will wreck their nerves.

Your resentment and anger may not hurt the other person but will have spoiled your own life because those thoughts sap away your energy. Every time you get into a fit of anger you lose hundreds and thousands of red corpuscles and the body can become anemic. So, for our own good, it's not worth it. Every thought that gives rise to hatred, resentment, fear, worry, lack of forgiveness, and so on can affect your health.

Be loving, be compassionate, be sympathetic. Those who hurt others are suffering themselves. Serve those who are suffering. That is real Yoga, real love, sympathy, mercy, and compassion. Swami Sivanandaji always said: "Be good, do good, be kind, be compassionate." How simple it is.

So, live to serve others and be kind and compassionate to one and all. These qualities should make you a fit instrument to understand and to realize your own spirit as the image of God in you. With this understanding, the whole world will be your friend and you will truly be blessed.

Chapter 6: The Pure in Heart

Blessed are the pure in heart, for they shall see God.

Sri Swami Satchidananda:

Out of all the Beatitudes, this one really caught me, really won my heart, for so many years. It contains such a beautiful teaching, such a simple truth. Jesus could have said something else from the mountain top like, "Blessed are the people who build big churches. Blessed are those who make beautiful golden crosses."

He never said anything like that because to see God you don't need to build churches, make golden images, burn thousands of candles, convert thousands of people, or print millions of Bibles and distribute them. Anybody can do these things.

If you have money you can convert the whole world. How many people who were in third world countries got converted, not because they wanted that religion or wanted God. They got converted because they were given food, schooling, a job, or some material comforts. If you build a school and give them education, they will come. If you give them nice clothing, fine. If you give them good jobs, well and good. They won't worry about what label you want to put on them. Yesterday they were Hindus, probably hungry. Today, their stomachs are satisfied, only their label has changed to "Christians." It doesn't matter to them because the stomach is happy now. But that is not the real idea behind religion and scriptures.

Even in yogic terms, Jesus could have said, "Blessed are the people who do half-an-hour of headstand every day." Some of the dolphins do better Yoga postures. But who shall see God? The pure in heart. Jesus didn't say anything about all the rituals, techniques, and spiritual practices you do. He didn't give any requirement about how many times you should visit your church, how much money you should have, or how you should look. No, because it's immaterial what you do. Who worries about that? The question is: Are you pure in heart? That means, is your mind calm and clean? Are you tranquil? Do you have equanimity? If the answer is yes, then you will see God.

And that's Yoga, too. Just this one sentence from Jesus has been put into two *sutras* by Patanjali. "Blessed are the pure in heart" has the same meaning as, "*Yogas chitta vritti nirodhah.*" And "...they shall see God" is the same as, "*Tada drashtuh svarupe'vasthanam.*"

I don't worry about who translated whom. Probably the historians will say that Patanjali lived many years before. We don't need to worry about that because they gave this same teaching in different language. *Chitta vritti nirodhah* is purity of mind. A mind filled with *vrittis* or waves is turbulent. If you calm the turbulence and make the mind quiet, then you will rest in your *svarupa*, your True Nature, which is

God: *Tada drashtuh svarupe'vasthanam.* You see yourself as God when you can make your mind calm and clean. That is what Yoga says.

"Blessed are the pure in heart." Jesus did not say "Blessed are the pure in head." The heart should be pure and then you will use the heart to develop compassion and universal love so there is no barrier—no "I, me, mine," but only "ours." The whole world becomes our home. Everybody is our own family member.

If we are really looking for peace on earth, that's the only way. Let us learn to love each other as one family. How? The only way is to develop a beautiful heart—a loving, generous, compassionate heart filled with universal love.

Real love knows only one-way traffic. Love, Love, Love. Love for the sake of love because loving makes you happy. That happiness cannot be taken away by anybody. Pouring love onto hate is like pouring water on fire. The heart has a tendency to melt. Just allow it to melt. This is the easiest way to approach God, to see God, as Jesus puts it. Have compassion, understanding, forgiveness, love, selflessness—all these beautiful qualities come from the heart. When you meditate on the heart, imagine that God is there making your heart beat, that God is the beat, and is the movement of loving energy within you. The heart must pray, not the lips or the head.

The sacred heart is a secret heart. If you love God more, you draw God more. As your love for God develops, you come to see and love your Self, which is also your neighbor's Self, and which is God.

We may not be able to see God in our minds. We may not be able to unite in our minds, but we can unite in the heart. This is why Jesus emphasizes purity of heart. It is in the heart that we truly meet God, and each other, because the heart has a tendency to melt. It is the heart that expresses the beautiful qualities of compassion, understanding, and universal love. If the heads meet together, you know what will happen? They hit and only noise comes out. That is why we say that the head is a hard nut. Wherever you see people fighting over their differences, it is all due to the heads coming forward. Wherever you see the heart functioning, you see unity, you see coming together. So, the whole world should meet in heart.

We do have many differences in the bodies and minds and these can give rise to feeling, *I must get everything and it doesn't matter how much I poison you, the water, the air, and the earth. I must get everything I want and for me.*

When we put the individual first instead of the collective good, we won't hesitate to do anything and everything for a little gain.

But, instead of always dividing ourselves and fighting because of "my country, your country, my color, your color, my language, your language, your religion, my religion," we can realize the unity behind the diversity.

We can appreciate and celebrate our diversity rather than fighting in the name of differences. The only way to find peace is to embrace our differences, while going to the very heart, the very spirit, because in spirit we are one.

We are united in spirit and when we realize that, that is what is meant by spiritual realization. And where do we begin? We begin with ourselves.

So, if we just take this one teaching, this one Beatitude and follow it, we will have read the entire *Bible* and we will be leading a biblical, a universal life. Just this one sentence is enough.

There is a saying in a South Indian sacred text, "If you keep on running around in the name of pilgrimage, visiting holy places, taking holy baths, meeting holy men, all of a sudden one day you will come across somebody who will just give you a word." You will meet a *Satguru* who will just give you a word, that's all.

They won't even sit and give you a lecture. Once you receive that, humble yourself, be quiet and let the word work on you.

Think of how yogurt is made. A small amount of culture is added to a pot of milk. The milk need not do anything. All it has to do is just be quiet in a corner. The culture is dropped into the milk and goes to work on it. What does the culture do? Curdles the milk, is it not? The milk doesn't run around jumping, announcing that it got the culture. It just sits quietly and allows the culture to work on it.

When the milk becomes curdled it becomes solid and is no longer liquid. In the same way, when we let these truths of the Beatitudes and the *Yoga Sutras* sink into us, we get solidified, grounded in these truths.

Unfortunately, we may read these scriptures, we may quote sacred texts, but we don't go to the very depth of their meaning. This one Beatitude sums up all of the Beatitudes. Can a pure heart dislike anybody, hate anybody, deny anybody, be unrighteous, not show mercy, not be humble? Does God deny anybody? Even the one who denies God, God doesn't deny.

But often we are searching for God, but denying people for various reasons: *If that person doesn't have the same kind of belief or follow my religion then I judge and deny them. How then can I call myself pure? How can I call myself as compassionate as God?* That's why Jesus said, "Seek the Kingdom within." He didn't ask us to go out and do something there. It's all right to go out and look for inspiration, but there's no point in going "out there" without the "in here."

Remember: God's love is universal. Our love also should be universal and unconditional and that is the fruition of purity of heart. It is because of this purity of heart that real communion—not just something in a ritual, but the communion that has to happen within us— becomes possible.

Chapter 7: The Peacemakers

Blessed are the peacemakers, for they shall be called the children of God.

Sri Swami Satchidananda:

I am asked this question very often, "How can I find peace?" My answer is, "You don't have to find it. You have it, but don't disturb it." Everything that is beautiful and positive is already in you, as your essential nature.

Even though our very nature is peaceful, it may seem like something foreign in our hectic and chaotic modern world. If somebody is very peaceful we may wonder, *Are they on drugs or pretending to be "spiritual?"* We begin to suspect that person and wonder, *Why are they so peaceful? How can they be this peaceful?*

Everything seems to be "imitation" this or "imitation" that now. So even peace sounds like imitation. It is really true because we are in an artificial world. So even the very original, natural things look like they are artificial. We should be asking ourselves, *Why is it that I am not experiencing that peace that is always there?* And this is what true peacemakers do: they are the ones who first realize the peace within themselves and then they just move around inspiring others by their example. They don't fight for peace or even preach peace. They just express peace in their way of life.

And how can we realize our peace? As I said before, by keeping the mind calm and by leading a dedicated life. These are the people who fit to be peacemakers.

However, somehow I feel that they should call themselves the "peacekeepers," rather than the "peacemakers." Peace is not something that you *make*. The peace was already made long, long before. When that Cosmic Awareness that we call "God" desired to create the world that God, as peace, created the world with peace. So the peace is already there and we have to keep it as peace and we should not disturb it. Peace and God are one and the same. So, peacekeeping and God-keeping are the same.

In order to be a peacekeeper, you should ask this question whenever you feel disturbed: *Since when have I been disturbed? And, what happened to cause the disturbance?* Then you will find the answer. Since the minute that you wanted something for yourself—a selfish desire, a selfish want—you lost your peace. *I wanted this. Now I am working toward that, and as I am working toward that, I am building an anxiety about whether I will get it or not? And if I get it, I'm excited. Hey, I got it!*

Excitement is another form of disturbance. That's why when you get too excited; you will lose your mind. Many times, people become insane when they get excited too much. There are also news reports of people who collapsed—some even died of a heart attack—after they were told that they had won several million dollars in the lottery.

Over-excitement is the positive form of disturbing one's peace. Depression is the negative form of disturbing one's peace. So when you are craving something and you get it, your peace is disturbed. When you don't get something you want, you are depressed, which is another form of disturbance.

It's not that there's something wrong with wanting things, especially if they are for the benefit of ourselves and others, but if we continually run after things thinking they will bring us happiness, we will only be disappointed at one point or another.

Another important thing to recognize is that even the excitement that came by getting something doesn't last. Within a few minutes, you'll be worried not to lose what you got: *I got it now, how can I keep it? I don't want to lose it.*

This is all based on the idea that I want to get something for myself. Even the Buddha said that the cause of all suffering is because of craving and aversion. So, we must be aware of these things and how they affect our inner peace and contentment.

Selfless acts will never disturb our minds. If you want to see this for yourself, try this out: Any time you feel disturbed, if you really analyze the situation, you will find that you have done something for your sake, with a selfish motive behind it. And that is what caused the disturbance.

Experiment further and try to do things without selfishness, but for others. See what happens. Take a day, or even a week, and see if you can minimize self-centered thoughts and actions.

It is possible to even live for the sake of others, eat for the sake of others. You can sleep for the sake of others. You can breathe for the sake of others. The *Bhagavad Gita* says: T*yagat shantir anantaram*, which means "The dedicated ever enjoy peace."

For such people peace is always experienced. It is only people like this who can really contribute something to the peace and harmony of the world.

I know many of you might ask, "What does this have to do with being a peacemaker, with world peace? I thought that the Swami will talk about how to be peacemakers in the world, as Jesus said we should do." In a way, I am talking about being a peacemaker and about world peace.

But, each person who wants to be a peacemaker needs to first take care of their own peace. How often we hear the announcement from the airplanes: "Put on your own oxygen mask first and then help others." If we don't find our own peace, if we don't take care of our inner peace, then what good are we to others?

We are all cells of the cosmic body. Every cell has to be healthy in order for the whole body to be healthy. As such, every individual is equally important. So peace should begin with individual minds. Otherwise we cannot go out and "make" peace. Once you have found your own peace, then you will be in a good position to help your neighbor in finding their peace and that's how we become peacemakers and inspire others to do the same. Gradually the peace expands.

You see, it is not only that charity begins at home, peace also begins at home. And remember, to experience the kingdom of God within, the previous Beatitude asks us to purify our hearts.

Once you have found that kingdom within you, then you will be able to see God's kingdom outside of you also. You will be in a position to understand the Cosmic plan and to be an effective peacemaker. Our first and foremost duty is to experience the peace, that God within us. Realize that peace first and then you will know what to do and how to serve as a peacemaker.

Once we sacrifice our selfishness, we become unlimited—world citizens, universal beings. We are no longer limited to our own life, our own country. We are not limited to our country, creed, color, language. Then we learn to love everybody as ourselves. This is what is meant by "universal love" and "love thy neighbor as thyself."

The whole world can shout for peace, but shouting cannot bring peace. Peace is not experienced by shouting but by finding the peace within, by not disturbing one's own peace. And then as a peaceful person, if you simply walk into a room, you will exude peace and all those who have eyes will recognize that.

They will come and ask you, "Hey, you seem to be so peaceful. What is the secret? How can I find peace and be a peacemaker?" In this way, we can become really useful people. Then, we truly will be peacemakers, peacekeepers, and what a blessing that will be.

Chapter 8: The Persecuted

Blessed are those who are persecuted for righteousness sake, for theirs is the kingdom of heaven.

Sri Swami Satchidananda:

In the fourth Beatitude, Jesus told us that those who thirst after righteousness will be filled and we know what righteousness means. Now, Jesus adds more to this teaching: that those who are righteous and stand for righteousness may be persecuted, but they will find that theirs is the kingdom of heaven. What is meant by "the kingdom of heaven?"

In the next chapter of St. Matthew (6:33), Jesus talks about this kingdom when he says, "Seek ye first the kingdom of God, and all these things shall be added unto you." The kingdom of heaven and kingdom of God are the same: the spiritual realm within you where the hidden treasure lies.

What is the hidden treasure? It is the spiritual heart within which we find "the peace that passeth all understanding;" the peace of God that is our True Nature. Peace is the Divine in each and every one of us and it is beyond all mental concepts. It is beyond all understanding.

We cannot experience it by breaking our brains trying to figure out what it is all about. No, it is to be deeply felt and experienced; it is beyond words. How to experience it? By going within.

In the Tamil language, which is my native tongue from South India, the name for God is *Kaduval*, meaning "go within." It is both the name of God and the method to experience the kingdom.

In India, there are many names and forms of the one God. In South India, one of the most popular names is Muruga, which means: "The One who occupies a place inside." There is great meaning and wisdom in these ancient names of God.

So, Jesus is promising us that if we are righteous, and even if we are persecuted, the kingdom will be ours. In truth, it already *is* ours, because it is our essential nature. Yet, we may not recognize this or feel that always because, as Jesus told us earlier, a pure heart is required in order to see God—in yogic terms: to see ourselves as God.

Now, while this teaching about persecution may not be easy to swallow, the truth is that in order to see our True Self, we need a clean and clear mirror. You are the Seer who wants to see itself. How? Even in the case of your physical face, if I ask if you have ever seen it, you have to say no, because it is the face that sees.

The face itself is the seer or the subject. What it sees in the mirror is its image, the seen, or the object. If the mirror is curved, wavy, or concave, will you be able to see your true face? No. It will appear to be awful—too big, too high, full of waves, and so distorted. Will you be worried seeing this? Will you run to the hospital? No! You will immediately know something is wrong with the mirror and that you are seeing a distorted reflection.

Only if the mirror is perfectly smooth and clean will it give you the true reflection. Only then can you see your face as it is. In the same way, the Seer, or true you, reflects in the mind which is your mirror.

Normally, you can't see the True Self because your mind is colored by so many distracting or disturbing thoughts and emotions. If the mind is distressed, you say, "I am distressed." If it's all polished and shining, "I am beautiful." That means you think you are your reflection in the mind.

If the mind has a lot of waves like the surface of a lake, you will be seeing a distorted reflection. If the water of the mental lake is muddy, you see your Self in a muddied way. To see the true reflection, see that the water is clean and calm and without any ripples.

That means that we need a calm, clear, and balanced mind to see the True Self. The mirror of the mind needs to be cleaned first in order for us to see who we are clearly and that requires purification—removing anything that obscures the mirror. However, without suffering there is no purification.

Whoever is interested in purifying themselves should accept suffering. If it comes, accept it. In yogic terminology we call this *tapas*. In the first *sutra* of the second chapter of the *Yoga Sutras*, Patanjali explains that the practice of *tapas* means to accept pain for purification.

Thiruvalluvar gives us the example of the process of purifying gold. How is golden ore purified so that you get 24-karat gold? By constantly melting it and relieving it from all unnecessary sediments and mixtures. The gold undergoes a lot of suffering. Every time the gold is heated, it is raised one more carat. The more you heat it, the more it shines. Why? Because all the dross, the unnecessary carbon and other things, is burnt out. Like that, the more you get heated by suffering the more you shine.

Tapas means "to burn." In other words, you are gently, sometimes urgently, roasted until you become ash. Then that's called *vibhuti* or holy ash. *Vibhuti* becomes a holy substance because it's totally burnt. That's why you have ash that is applied on Ash Wednesday in Christianity.

In Hinduism, holy ash is given to worshippers to apply to their foreheads at the temples during holy days and even daily. It's called *vibhuti* because it has all the great qualities of God. Everything that is beautiful, that is supreme is *vibhuti*.

You might be surprised to know what *vibhuti* is made from: cow dung! But it is no longer dung because all the dirty part is burned out of it completely so it becomes well-purified.

In the same way, suffering is helpful to us because it purifies our minds and hearts. When you have suffered enough, when you get burnt totally, then you no longer get trampled. As long as you are dung, you get trampled and thrown into the dung pit.

But when you get burnt, you become holy ash and you go onto the very forehead of a person. You are elevated to a great height, you are respected. So the benefit comes afterward. But until you are completely burnt you can't go to that spiritual height.

That reminds me of a wonderful parable. The Hindu temples are mostly built from granite. Inside the sanctum sanctorum, the *murti* (carved statue of a deity representing God) is made out of granite rock. And there is a granite step just in front of the altar. One day, a man was worshipping in front of the altar. There was nobody there except for him. All of a sudden, he heard a conversation that seemed to be going on between the *murti* and the granite step in front of it. The conversation went something like this:

"Hi, brother! How come you are getting all the decorations, all the offerings? Milk and honey are poured over you, you get decorated with nice jewels, flowers. Everyone comes and respects you. And this priest, even while he decorates you, he is stepping on me. Nobody seems to look at me. Even if they don't decorate me and respect me, can't they at least leave me alone instead of trampling on me? How come? Don't you know we were brothers? We were together, almost twins?"

The other one said, "Yes, my brother, I remember that. I can never forget it. We were together. We were one piece of granite when we were brought from the neighboring rock quarry. The sculptor started working and he split our one rock into two because it was too big for a *murti*. And he picked you up first and started shaping you into a beautiful image of God. He started hitting at you with his iron chisel and hammer.

"You became so furious that you shouted at him, yelled at him, 'How dare you do this? Leave me alone. I don't want to be hit like this.' And he thought that you are so unhappy, that you are possessed with a kind of ego or ignorance, so he just left you.

"Then he took the other half and started working on me. I kept quiet. I thought there must be some reason for it. After all, he is the one who brought me all the way to his workshop. I decided to let him do whatever he wanted. Of course it was really painful. Constantly, he rolled me over and over, he hit me day and night. He was sometimes even sitting on me and hitting me.

"But I waited and waited and after several months, all of a sudden, one day I saw myself as a beautiful *murti*. Then he put me inside this temple and the priest started doing all the decorations. When he put me here, I was a little too high for the priest to reach me, so the sculptor brought you for the priest to use as a stepping stone. So you were placed in front of me and that is why he is standing on you and pouring all the milk and honey on me."

"Oh, I see. Well, if I had known that, I would have accepted all those things; but I didn't."

"Well, I'm sorry, but it's too late. Just accept it. Pray for the next birth. And if somebody is hitting you, even if you don't know why, accept it. Be patient. Probably one day you will be respected. You'll be honored. You'll have all the decorations, all the festivities for yourself, just like me."

Did the sculptor work nicely, gently in order to make the granite rock into a beautiful image of God? No. And, in the same way, life gives us so many kinds of knocks and hits that purify and shape us. It is only by resistance we build strength, only through adversities and obstacles that our inner capabilities are brought forth.

We all have to go through pain and suffering as part of our spiritual growth. At some point in our lives, we also may be wrongly accused, even persecuted, for doing the right thing—or as Jesus said "for being righteous—so how to respond? At another point in his Sermon on the Mount, Jesus said to "turn the other cheek." As my Guru Swami Sivanandaji always said, "Bear insult, bear injury. This is the highest *sadhana*."

The kingdom of God can only come once the egoistic tendency goes, once we are free from the "I, me, and mine." When everything becomes "Thine," you are a true yogi, you are pure in heart, and you "shall see God," as Jesus promises. Then, you will experience your own True Nature as Super Consciousness.

Epilogue

As the *satsang* ended for the evening,
a devoted student came forward to ask Sri
Gurudev for a birthday blessing. They presented
Gurudev with a coconut and asked him to
break it, as a blessing.

Swami Satchidananda:

Does everyone know why the coconut is
broken? The coconut represents the human
mind. Since people mostly identify themselves
as the mind and talk in terms of that, they're
all more or less like coconuts. The coconut has
three parts. The upper surface, which is covered
with husk. Below the husk you see the hard
shell. Inside the shell you have a beautiful,
white kernel.

The husk represents the *tamasic* or lazy part
of the mind. The hard shell represents the *rajasic*
part, the restless, extremely active and egoistic

part of the mind. And the beautiful white kernel inside represents the *sattvic* or tranquil mind. That means that when the tranquil mind goes to one extreme it becomes restless. And if it goes to the other extreme, it becomes lazy. So you have all these three parts in the coconut.

Now here you see that I've been asked to break a coconut that is already husked. That means that even to approach a teacher for their blessing, the individual should remove their laziness first.

At this point, they realize that even after having removed the laziness it will be too hard for them to remove the egoistic part of their nature. Whatever they try, the ego gets into that. Sometimes the ego even gets into the so-called spiritual practices. Haven't you heard people saying, "I can stand on my head for half an hour. I do an hour of meditation every day?"

This itself is a form of egoism. It's hard to break that egoistic nature. Ultimately, having gotten tired of this struggle with the ego, the sincere student comes with all humility to a qualified teacher.

That teacher, with the sword of wisdom, gives the ego a hard hit. And then it breaks open to reveal a beautiful tranquil inner nature. And that's what the coconut symbolizes. So each one is a coconut. In the beginning, we were all very tender. But slowly, slowly we got hardened. The harder the nut, the bigger the ego. And now it's very difficult to break it. Once the ego shell is broken, you see a very beautiful kernel inside. It's very delicious. It's the kingdom of heaven within.

Breaking the coconut is more or less a symbolic act. We are wanting to relieve ourselves from the ego and to become pure in heart again. It's not only for the birthdays because normally you take a coconut to the temple and put it in the hands of the priest. And he cracks it open for you. This signifies that the teacher helps you to break your ego and bring out the beautiful you—the you to be offered to God. Then the priest gives you back the opened coconut and the tasty kernel is shared with everybody.

That means, once God sees your purity, accepts you completely, God gives you back to be distributed to everybody—your life becomes a beautiful and dedicated one, useful to everybody. That is the symbolic purpose of breaking a coconut.

Gurudev then prepared to crack the coconut, struck it, and it opened to reveal the beautiful purity of the inner coconut.

Gurudev wished this student a "Happy Birthday," and then gave them back the opened coconut.

The student cut the inner part into pieces, offered the first one to Gurudev, and then distributed the rest to each one in the gathering.

As the evening program drew to a close, Gurudev ended the *satsang* with the *Maha Mrityunjaya Mantra*, chanted three times for the well-being of all and a closing prayer for world peace:

Om tryambakam yajamahe
sugandhim pushti vardhanam
urvarukamiva bandhanan
mrityor mukshiya mamritat

We worship You, All-Seeing One.
Fragrant, You nourish bounteously.
From fear of death may You cut us free,
To realize Immortality.

Lokah samastah sukhino bhavantu

May the entire universe be filled with peace and joy, love and light.

Om Shanti Shanti Shanti

About Sri Swami Satchidananda

Sri Swami Satchidananda was one of the first Yoga masters to bring the classical Yoga tradition to the West. He taught Yoga postures to Americans, introduced them to meditation, vegetarian diet and a more compassionate lifestyle.

During this period of cultural awakening, iconic pop artist Peter Max and a small circle of his artist friends beseeched the Swami to extend his brief stop in New York City so they could learn from him the secret of finding physical, mental and spiritual health, peace and enlightenment.

Three years later, he led some half a million American youth in chanting *OM*, when he delivered the official opening remarks at the 1969 Woodstock Music and Art Festival and he became known as "the Woodstock Guru."

The distinctive teachings he brought with

him blend the physical discipline of Yoga, the spiritual philosophy of *Vedantic* literature and the interfaith ideals he pioneered.

These techniques and concepts influenced a generation and spawned a Yoga culture that is flourishing today. Today, over twenty million Americans practice Yoga as a means for managing stress, promoting health, slowing down the aging process and creating a more meaningful life.

The teachings of Swami Satchidananda have spread into the mainstream and thousands of people now teach Yoga. Integral Yoga® is the foundation for Dr. Dean Ornish's landmark work in reversing heart disease and Dr. Michael Lerner's noted Commonweal Cancer Help program.

Today, Integral Yoga Institutes, teaching centers and certified teachers throughout the United States and abroad offer classes and training programs in all aspects of Integral Yoga.

In 1979, Sri Swamiji was inspired to establish Satchidananda Ashram–Yogaville. Based on his teachings, it is a place where people of different faiths and backgrounds can come to realize their essential oneness.

One of the focal points of Yogaville is the Light Of Truth Universal Shrine (LOTUS). This unique interfaith shrine honors the Spirit that unites all the world religions, while celebrating their diversity. People from all over the world come there to meditate and pray.

Over the years, Sri Swamiji received many honors for his public service, including the Juliet Hollister Interfaith Award presented at the United Nations and in 2002 the U Thant Peace Award.

In addition, he served on the advisory boards of many Yoga, world peace and interfaith organizations. He is the author of many books on Yoga and is the subject of the documentary, *Living Yoga: The life and teachings of Swami Satchidananda*.

In 2002, he entered *Mahasamadhi* (a God-realized soul's conscious final exit from the body).

For more information, visit: www.swamisatchidananda.org

About Peter Max

Peter Max, one of America's most famous living artists, is also a pop culture icon. His bold colors, uplifting images and uncommon artistic diversity have touched almost every phase of American culture and have inspired many generations.

In 1966, Peter Max met Swami Satchidananda in Paris, invited him to America and helped him to found the Integral Yoga® Institute. Inspired by his friendship with Swami Satchidananda and the Yoga teachings he learned from him, Max created his signature style of cosmic scenes and characters, painted in bold, vibrant colors. It was among the most influential graphic sources of the 1960s and was often cited by journalists and art critics as the visual counterpart to the music of The Beatles.

Cited as "America's Painter Laureate," Peter Max has painted portraits of six U.S. Presidents and his impressionistic paintings of the Statue

of Liberty and American flag art are on display in Presidential Libraries and U.S. Embassies.

Max's work in portraiture has extended to world leaders (Mikhail Gorbachev, Nelson Mandela, H. H. The Dalai Lama, Dr. Martin Luther King, Jr.), CEOs (Richard Branson, Sumner Redstone) and major figures in the world of sports and entertainment.

His exhibitions have had record-smashing attendance at such venues as the de Young Museum, the Hermitage Museum and the Moscow Academy of Art. And, although he has produced major work in traditional media, such as canvas, paper, bronze and ceramic, he has also demonstrated how fine art can enrich non-traditional media, such as a U.S. postage stamp, a Continental Airlines' super jet and a 600-foot stage set for the 1999 Woodstock Music Festival.

As official artist for more major cultural events than any other contemporary artist,

Max has championed the causes of peace, ecology, democracy, human and animal rights and charity—confirming that he is not only one of America's most prolific living artists, but also one of the most relevant.

For more information, please visit: petermax.com